MW00881756

ISBN-13: 978-1533021588
ISBN-10:1533021589

I am Tooki

A BOOK ABOUT BEING YOU

Written and Illustrated by Jin Palmer
Edited by Erika Palmer

How amazing—you are the only you
in the world.

I am Tooki, the only me in the world.

We are *all* unique,
and that is wonderful.

You love playing on a swing.

I love sliding down a tree.
We find different things fun and merry.

You like popping bubbles.

I like hearing a pig's giggles.
We find different things funny.

We are *all* one of a kind.

Isn't that interesting?

Do what *you* love.
Nobody can do that for you but *you*.
Do it as much as you can every day.

Some of us are small, and some of us are big. Soon enough, you will grow big and strong.

When you do grow big and strong, remember that you are still the special you. Just more.

Go ahead.
Create your own story anywhere you
want to.

You might find new places inviting.

You are *always* with the special you.
Isn't that exciting?

The world is a big place, with seven billion people and counting.

The universe is a bigger place,
with one hundred billion galaxies and
growing.

There is only one you,
and there is only one me.
It is infinitely special to be us.

We are *all* one of a kind, made of the stars in the sky. Isn't that astounding?

Be kind to all, and keep on shining.

We are *all* unique and special.

Remember it every day.

About the Author

Jin Palmer is a mom of three vibrant children and feels passionate about teaching the concept of self-compassion to young children.
After having her first child, she realized that every individual on this planet is somebody's child, and that makes all of us very special. This seemingly obvious but profound realization changed her perspective on life. This book is a result of her mission to spread the message of self-compassion to young children. Jin loved painting with watercolors as a child. She decided to pick up her paintbrush again as she had a strong desire to express her passion for this book. She hoped to capture the joyful little things in life as a parent—the adorably tiny feet that are gently crossed; the warmth of soft, round fingers; and the complete openness only children naturally possess.
Her daughter, Erika (currently a fourth grader), graciously played the role of editor in chief during the creation of this book. Erika enjoys being immersed in reading every day and loves writing about fictional characters.

Author Acknowledgement

Thank you, readers.
I am so grateful that you picked up *I am Tooki*.
I hope that you feel the message of self-compassion is as important as I felt when I was creating this book. I would love to hear from you. Please visit www.iamtooki.com

Thank you, friends and family.
We created this book with lots of love and joy. You made our journey even more amazing with your love and support. Special thanks to Mom, Dad, Brad, Erika, Yong, Justin, Marcus, Ray, Teri, Sherri, Laurie and *me*.